MERELY A MATTER OF COLOUR

A donation from the profits of this anthology will be made
to the Uganda Asian Relief Fund.

THE UGANDA ASIAN ANTHOLOGY

MERELY A MATTER OF COLOUR

Edited by E. A. Markham and Arnold Kingston

"Q" BOOKS

"Q" BOOKS *(Publishers)* LTD.
16 Hillersdon Avenue
Edgware, Middx.

First published 1973

ISBN 0 9502982 0 4 cloth
ISBN 0 9502982 1 2 paper

Printed in Great Britain
by Freedman Bros. Ltd
London.

"It was merely a matter of colour. It didn't matter any more what you were, or who you were, or what you thought, or how you felt — all that had ceased to matter, only your colour mattered. Even before you had said one word, the colour of your skin had spoken already and it had spoken loudly; it had spoken even when you were still far away in the distance, to establish what would seem to be the truth about you, the whole truth and nothing but the truth."

Jagjit Singh

ACKNOWLEDGMENTS

The publishers gratefully acknowledge the previous publication of the following works:

Merely a Matter of Colour by Jagjit Singh in *Ghala July 1968,* East Africa Journal.

From Citizen to Refugee by Mahmood Mamdani, Frances Pinter Ltd.

Sweet Scum of Freedom by Jagjit Singh in *African Theatre* (Henderson), Heinemann Educational Books Ltd.

The Leader by Peter Nazareth from the novel *In a Brown Mantle,* East Africa Literature Bureau.

Portrait of an Asian as an East African by Jagjit Singh in *Poems From East Africa* (Cook & Rubadiri), Heinemann Educational Books Ltd.

Acknowledgment is also made to the BBC for *Sweet Scum of Freedom* by Jagjit Singh.

CONTENTS

PREFACE

In November 1972, when we came together with "Q" Books on this project our main aim was to present a collection of writings by Uganda Asians that reflected their individual thoughts and feelings. It was not, necessarily, our intention to produce their side of the story, or an indictment of the peoples of Uganda as a whole. In selecting contributions our main criterion was simply, that the work should be of merit and of interest. No doubt there are and will be books giving a comprehensive account of the origins of the Uganda Asian crisis, books on the policies of General Idi Amin, books on the traumas of exile and life in the resettlement camps. MERELY A MATTER OF COLOUR is not primarily concerned with these topics, although as can be expected, the contributors have been strongly affected by recent events to the extent that their experiences have influenced some of their stories and poems.

We embarked on this project because we felt that the impression was being created that the exiled Asians were 'a problem to be solved — a foreign element to be tolerated'. This emphasis, in our opinion, was and is wrong. What is now needed is to allow people to present their own image in their own way. The gap that has been created between the Uganda Asians and the British public cannot be bridged merely by statistics published by the Uganda Resettlement Board. The gap can only and will only be bridged at the grass-roots level — people to people.

We hope this book is one step in that direction.

We would like to express our thanks to Tuku Mukherjee, Jagjit Singh and H. M. Sheard for helping to contact some of the contributors, to Richard and Trish Porte, Eric Moonman and Maurice

11

Miller MP for their support and advice, and finally to D. R. Hallet and G. Baumgard of "Q" Books for their assistance in editing and compiling this book.

E.A.M.
A.K.

MERELY A MATTER OF COLOUR

MERELY A MATTER OF COLOUR
Jagjit Singh

It was Saturday morning — bright and brilliant and warm, like any other day of any other week in any other African city. People strolled about brisk and business-like down the streets of Kampala with the sun labouring higher and higher up the sky while white clouds sighed and drifted apart to let the rays of light filter onto the city below. Fortunately, the Government, unlike elsewhere, had been liberal enough not to ban the mini-skirt and in the tempting luke warm heat of the morning, pair after pair of sex hungry thighs strolled nakedly down the streets, each skirt more daring, tighter and higher up than the previous ones; each flapping a scent perfume of its own creation. Men who had lost their equilibrium stopped, turned round and stared long and hard at the pink, black and brown goddesses of sex who walked by. Everything else was natural enough. Newspapers lay on the pavements like every other day, but few people paid much attention to the black headlines: 'THREE MORE HANGED IN RHODESIA. SMITH HAS NEW POLICY FOR AFRICANS', which seemed almost out of place and trivial. All the same the headlines were bold and their stark-nakedness rose and struck you in the eye each time you cared to look. But you didn't care to look much and there was no horror, no sorrow, no protest on the faces of the people passing by. They drifted about in their usual lifeless way, the newspaper in their hands, with a faraway, uncommitted look in their eyes.

At the corner, the black Mercedes came to a stop and the white woman got out. She smiled at the black man behind the steering wheel and said, 'Kale, Weraba.' Then she smiled again and added, 'Onojja ku sawaki?'

The African pulled up his shirt sleeve and consulted the expensive-looking watch.

'Ku sawa musamvu?' he asked.

'O.K. That's fine. I'll wait at the Post-Office. And don't keep me waiting like last time.'

'No, of course not . . . I'll be dead on time.'

And she closed the door softly and began walking away, swaying gently to the left and to the right in the usual feminine way, towards the market. He looked at her backside gliding away like a bird before he released the brake and let the car roll down the road. He smiled at her terribly foreign Luganda accent. She had insisted she wanted to learn his language.

'But, you don't have to,' he had said. 'I speak English and that's enough, isn't it?'

But she had replied, 'No, it isn't, ' with absolute finality. 'How do I know you aren't saying all the bad things about me when you talk to your people in your own language?'

'But heavens, there isn't anything bad about you. What *would* I want to tell them anyway?'

'Oh lots of things . . . like how I'm never on time for anything and how I'm never reliable and how I never keep my promises. Or like that time we nearly quarrelled when you wrote me a bundle of letters and I never replied which was because I never *got* the bundle of letters since I had moved elsewhere but you thought I *had* them and that I didn't write back because I didn't care and so the next time we met you were terribly upset and I didn't even know about it and *that* made you more upset. Remember that?'

'No, I forget horribly fast! But anyway I don't hold that against you any more.'

'Or that time I had my hair cut short and you were furious because you liked it long and didn't want it short.'

'Well, you're the lord of your hair. I'm not. All the same I still like it long. Anyway I'd want people to know you were a wonderful wife and not a piece of trash picked in the bar so why would I tell them anything bad about you?'

'Oh I don't know. You're making it more complicated. Maybe it's

16

just that I don't feel at ease you knowing one more language than me. So I want to learn it too. It's not criminal, is it?'

'Well no . . . but why didn't you say so before. If it's an inferiority complex, I'll teach you right away.'

And she had said, well you could put it that way and so he had put it that way and started teaching her Luganda.

But of course, it wasn't only a complex — come to think of it, it wasn't that at all. She just thought it was nice knowing one more language—it made her feel more a part of the world and any time she felt like it, she could take a deep breath, let her breasts rise skywards, throw back her head and declare, 'I speak eight languages' and before the rudiments of a tiny smile could form on her red lips, she would add quickly, 'or at least bits here and there.' Besides it did help her a lot while she was at the market. She never could make out the difference when the man behind the stall said twenty, thirty or forty cents for something or other she wanted to buy. All the figures sounded so much the same to her and so she would just hand him a shilling and trust the fellow would give back the correct change.

She took off her sunglasses and walked into the market. A small boy who had faithfully followed her all the way from the parking space, finally plucked up enough courage, touched her basket and mumbled something shyly, half expecting to be turned away. She understood what he wanted and let him carry her basket while she picked the fruits. Now that she did speak bits and pieces of the language, she felt more at ease. She'd stop here and there looking at the fruits, then she'd pick up something and ask the price. If it turned out to be a figure she hadn't learnt yet, she'd point to her fingers and ask how much it was that day. Of course she thought it was funny but she didn't seem to mind the man behind the counter who seemed to be laughing at her.

Soon she noticed that the boy was weighed down by the basket and for fear she might not be able to carry so heavy a weight herself, she decided she had bought enough.

Just then somebody touched her arm from behind and she turned

17

around in surprise.

'Hello, I thought I'd surprise you.'

She looked at the smartly dressed African girl and said, 'Why yes, you surprised me dear. Not so badly though . . . I'm used to it now.'

The girl smiled. 'That's what we call adapting to the new environment in biology.'

'Oh you do?' And in a moment, they had eased themselves out of the crowds and were now standing at the corner. 'Now you'll be telling me it has something to do with the missing link and evolution and all the rest of it too!'

The girl twitched her nose for a while thoughtfully. Then she nodded her head briskly. 'Well, it does actually,' she said, 'but that's a different story. If you didn't get bored so easily I *would* give you the *details* sometime . . . but of course you'd much rather talk about interior decorating, so I needn't bother.'

'But interior decorating does have something to do with environment, doesn't it Jane?'

'Well, yes definitely . . . but . . . '

'And the colour motif affects adaptability too?'

'Yes, but you see again . . . '

'Well there you are then : interior decorating does have a place in biology. If it has an effect on *both* environment *and* adaptability, where else would you place it then?'

The girl smiled, wishing she hadn't walked into such an obvious trap so easily. Then, as if adapting herself to the new environment, she said, 'Well yes, I think you're right. Come to think of it, it's the latest branch of biology!'

'Oh really?'

Then they smiled knowingly at each other, more as a sign of self-congratulation at the remarkably smooth progress of their rather stupid little game. The boy carrying the basket fidgeted uncomfortably trying to keep the flies away from the wound on his leg. Around them, people were squeezing in and out of the market and because it looked awkward to stand there talking shop, she looked at her watch.

'Do you remember I was telling you about going abroad? Well, I did get admission to Cambridge University, I got the scholarship too! Should be moving out soon.'

'Oh, isn't that simply marvellous?' was all she could say. And then she remembered the dress she was making for the girl. 'Remember that dress I was making for you? Well I've nearly completed it. Why don't you drop in for tea this evening and then you can have a look at the dress too. Besides I want to know all about when you're going away.'

She said she would love to and could she come at five in the evening?

'But of course, what's there to stop you? I'll be waiting for you.'

Nice kid, she thought as she walked away to the end of the parking space. The "nice kid" was her husband's sister. She took the basket. It *is* heavy, she said to herself, giving the African boy a shilling. Maybe she shouldn't be carrying such heavy weights. The doctor had told her it was risky since she was pregnant. But she told herself that the weight wasn't much really.

By now it was fairly warm and as she walked into the main street amidst a greeting of the hooting and screeching of cars, she felt squashed by people on all sides. She had never liked walking through thick crowds — there was always someone banging into her. Sometimes she got the feeling that some people banged their shoulders into her deliberately, just to touch her. Sometimes she did bang into someone herself and then she had to pull herself together, get back her balance and apologise to the unfortunate fellow. And she would walk on, cursing herself silently for being so English as to say sorry every time something silly happened.

Today, with a basket full of vegetables she certainly didn't feel like being jostled around.

Suddenly she slowed down and then stopped dead for she thought she heard something — something like a shuffling of innumerable feet sweeping towards her, and a chanting of many voices, now shrill, now rumbling and demanding, biting deeper into the eardrums than the hooting and the screeching of the cars. She stood on her toes, raising her high heels higher still and holding her hand over her eyebrows as she tried to stretch her eyesight further than the shiny glare of the sun would allow. Then she saw the streets ahead filled with the thick mass of African students, clothed in red gowns sweeping down the roads and the traffic began to fade out. She thought there was something threatening about the advancing crowd, like the onslaught of angry red ants that left nothing decent untouched on the way. And yet she felt rooted to the ground, unable to move and she stared at other people around her and saw them all standing still too.

Now that the long lines of the angry and inflamed youths had come much nearer her, she saw there were a few Asians and Europeans too, clothed in red gowns, screaming; with sticks in their outstretched arms, they gestured in a funny almost hysterical way. But somehow she felt the Asians and the Europeans weren't really serious; they were so few in fact, she told herself, that if you were to squash the whole crowd and flick their limbs one over the other, you would hardly tell the colour of their blood in the heap of useless limbs, for it would soon become dry, black ... But no, it wasn't really fair, she thought, everything about Africa was black; well, except the grass that was green and the sky that was blue and white. But then the grass and the sky didn't belong to anybody, did they? — though people did put up claims of course. Which was irrelevant really, because people were so irrational anyway. Always had been. Always would be. The point was, countries shouldn't belong to anybody either. But that too had become irrelevant because countries always *had* belonged to people. Always would. Which was all because people were so stupid really. But then, she thought, if countries *had* to belong to somebody, let them belong to half-castes ...

And yet sometimes she would feel tormented by the thought that her own son, when he was a grown up man, might feel the way she now did, perhaps much more. What if he belonged neither to one world nor to the other? What if he felt cast into a vacuum with his roots uprooted, left in the different winds to dry and wither and die away, as he swayed about, back and forth from one extreme world to the other. This sad note often lingered in her heart. 'What then?' an inner voice would ask. But as time had gone by, she had felt much happier and so much less inhibited. She felt a strange kind of happiness at belonging to everybody, at being able to be in the midst of everybody and everything and not feel at anytime that there was something special about *her* kind of people. And, she had told herself, she would bring up her son with such tender care and love and understanding that he was bound to feel proud of himself. At least he would feel so much more tolerant than other people were. And all this went for the other child too that she was now pregnant with.

She felt somebody push her and she was immediately jolted out of her pensiveness. She looked at the man who had disturbed her but the fellow was beyond caring; he stood on his toes, a strange expression on his face, and his neck craned for a better view of the demonstration.

By now the red gowns, swinging through the streets, were fully inflamed, burning from top to bottom in an ugly, uncontrollable fury as the students flung their arms in fierce uninhibited gestures. With each step they took — threatening steps, she thought — the angry voices, denouncing and condemning the injustices of what seemed to be all white men in general, became louder and louder and stabbed into her breast with a strange and curious bitterness.

She kept at bay and tried to read the placards the students were carrying. 'Hang Smith and Wilson . . . NOW!' She thought that was tremendously funny; what's the hurry, why not keep them in gaol for a while? That's what *they* always do to the blacks that they hang. Always have done. Always would. And then there were others like 'Humbled Bulldog, It Is Later Than You Think!'

She didn't know what to think. It's probably true, she thought. 'Devalue sterling, Mr Wilson, not lives.' She breathed deeply. Is that what the Empire had come to? Incredible! But things happen she thought. Even though they ought not to. She looked at another placard. 'Sonofabitch Smith, We'll paint Salisbury RED with your

BLOOD.' Sounds reasonable enough, she said to herself. And as she turned away, she again felt sick of the violence and the fury that was passing her by. Each time the students shouted something evil, the winds swept voices towards her and she felt uneasy and curiously unbalanced.

Here are my husband's people condemning my people, she thought sadly. Condemning me too and so many others who have never been infected with the disease of my race. They're spitting in my face too but what fault is it of mine? What a marvellous legacy, this, for my sons! What lessons shall I teach them, what antiseptic for these young hearts and souls so much infected with a hate that will surely destroy them. How ironical!

Suddenly she wished she hadn't come to town today. From the other side of the town she heard the unmistakable noise of a crash — like the dull thud of a sharp stone slapping glass and shattering it into a million fragments. She watched, shocked, unable to move, mute like a stone. The brakes had long since been applied and the car had skidded to a halt. Someone pulled out the white driver and hurled him over the pavement. There was blood already on the man's face — blood from the sharp-edged pieces of glass from his shattered windscreen.

'No!' she hissed to herself. 'Stop it you beastly bastards.' And she clutched tight to her basket. But that didn't stop them.

She didn't want to watch anymore and yet she couldn't close her eyes. Just a few yards away she could see a man furiously whacking the back of a helpless woman, with a green stick he had freshly cut from a tree. And she heard the chilling screams of the woman as she fought desperately with her delicate arms to beat off the savage blows. At last she had managed to find the arm of her little six year old girl and had dragged her away from the road and into the crowds. She had a brief glance at the little white girl, wailing loudly one hand over her eyes, the other holding her torn dress together. And she felt helpless with sorrow. Pain stabbed at her heart — the pain you feel when someone sticks a knife in you for the crimes of a man who lived next door to you nearly a decade ago. She stretched her shoulders to ease the pain but the pain shot upwards to her neck and she felt a tight knot under her chin and she felt her lips quivering and her eyeballs swimming in a cupful of tears. And she hoped desperately the cup would not overflow because she didn't want tears rushing down her cheeks and spoiling her make-up.

This is no place for me, she thought and she began to press deeper and deeper into the thick crowds behind her for safety, the thick shield of human flesh which before now she had always avoided. But the shield itself was thick and solid now and she knew she couldn't possibly break into it.

Then as she was fighting her way into the crowd, she saw one of the black men in the red gowns staring at her, shouting something and pointing an accusing finger at her.

'Come out, white bastards, let's see how we hang you!' he shouted.

Suddenly she felt more frightened than ever and fought desperately to disappear into the crowds.

And it happened just then. The thing happened. The thing she had felt all along *would* happen and all the hiding behind the crowds was useless. The thing she had hoped so desperately wouldn't happen. And it had happened!

Someone behind kicked hard at her basket and as her arm shot forward, she let go the basket and the vegetables went flying and fell right at the feet of the passing demonstration. She lost her balance and was fumbling awkwardly. Then she heard laughter behind her and, simultaneously, she felt somebody's hands on her arm. She screamed and kicked him on the legs. Then she looked into the painfully cruel, harsh and mocking expression on the man's face. It was the same man who had stared at her, pointing an accusing finger and who had shouted something obscene just a moment ago. For the brief interlude that she saw the gloating expression in his eyes, she lost all hope and before she could even scream again, she knew there was no longer anything under her feet and that she had been pulled right out of the crowd. She felt herself flying — the man had let go her arm and she fell with full force. Instinctively she brought her hands to protect her head and as she did so, she felt blood on her face. Just then someone threw a large stone at the windscreen of a car parked nearby and the fragments hit her naked legs. Amidst her agonised screams of pain, she felt somebody walking over her legs and the pieces of glass bit deep into her flesh. She screamed again — like the final scream of death. And then she felt something drop on her head . . .

She never knew what had happened to her after she fainted. She had lain with the vegetables scattered all over the road and then she had fainted. Only when the angry tide had passed away had some-body bothered to find out how she was. As it turned out, it was one of her husband's friends who first saw her lying on the road. Being a practical man, he hadn't spent much time wishing this hadn't hap-pened to her. He had lifted her swiftly into his strong arms and seeing she had fainted, had driven her straight to the hospital. Then he had phoned her husband.

Her husband had just been getting ready to leave when the phone rang.

'I'm sorry John,' the friend said. 'There's been an accident. Your wife's slightly hurt.'

'What accident?' her husband had asked thinking she was always so careful.

'Something to do with the students' demonstration.'

'*What* demonstration?'

'Didn't you know? That damned thing about the hangings in Rhodesia.'

'But . . . but my wife's . . . ' And he stopped. He couldn't say more. But my wife's pregnant, he had wanted to cry out.

Not knowing how to interpret the abrupt silence over the phone, his friend had said, 'Look, I'm still at the hospital. I'll wait for you. Why don't you rush over?'

His hands shook and his legs too were beginning to feel unsure of themselves as John put down the phone and rushed out of his office.

He stood looking down at her. Her lips were swollen and there were bruises all over her cheeks. He bit his lips and instinctively touched her hair and brought them over her forehead. Then he drew back in horror.

He had met her in Canada while he was a student there. The meeting had been as romantic and original as she was. They had just happened to bump into each other at the right angle corner on the Campus, somewhat in the manner of those love-at-first-sight stories. It had been a head-on collision and as usual, under such circumstances, both of them had let go of their files and the papers had scattered all over.

'I'm so *terribly* sorry,' he had said.

She shook her head and the blonde hair came tumbling over her face and she pushed it away from her sea blue eyes and said, 'Oh well, it's fifty per cent my fault.'

He had started gathering her papers and while he was doing that, she had started gathering his. As it turned out, both of them finished sorting out the papers simultaneously. She smiled at the awkwardness of the situation.

'I hope you aren't hurt,' he mumbled.

'No, I'm all right.'

There had been silence and then she had said, 'You might as well tell me your name.'

He had done that. 'Yours?'

When she told him her name, he asked, 'How do you spell it? . . . L-e-i-g-h?'

'No,' she told him.

'Well, then L-e-e?'

'No,' she repeated curling her lips into a tiny smile and stretching the 'o' of the 'no' so long, one would think they had been friends for years.

'Well then, how?'

'Don't you want to try any more?'

He shook his head.

She had smiled triumphantly and breathed deeply. Then said, 'L-i. That's how!'

'Oh, how come?' he asked.

She had started walking her way and there was nothing he could do but go together with her, even though that meant he had to go back the way he had just come rushing from.

'Well, it's like this,' she began. 'I'm mixed breed. My dad was a pure American but my mom had an American father and a Japanese mother and I was born in China!'

'Oh!' he had said, surprised at her ancestry. 'So you have more of America in you than Asia, right?'

'Well, yes . . . But I was born in Asia, so that sort of balances it out, doesn't it?'

And in spite of himself, he had felt attracted to her. With her penetrating navy blue eyes and the sweetly perfumed, wavy hair and her tall, solid figure he *had* to admit that she looked beautifully striking.

Perhaps his father had been right, but that didn't really matter right now because he hated his father too. He remembered how he had written back home, explaining that he wanted to marry this girl. Of course it had all been done very cautiously. To begin with, he had just sent them a photo of two or three other friends besides the two of them. Much to his fury, nobody at home had bothered to ask who she was. So sometime later, seeing that the preliminary talks had met such miserable failure, he had decided on direct negotiations. But that plan too met its miserable end. His father, who was not much of a reader or a writer — nor a diplomat for that matter — had been furious and had got somebody to write the wayward son a telling letter on the virtues of the family pedigree, hitherto unblemished. It had all been very clear: his father didn't want his son going around with white women; he had already chosen a bride for him; people of different colours and different nations and backgrounds and lan-

26

guages should never mix together so intimately as to compromise in bed; the cultural gaps were too big!

But at last he had returned back to Africa with his wife and their child. And his father had taken one deep and painful look at the child and boiling with disapproval and shame at the impurity of his flesh, had said, 'Was this what you left my home for — to go out and bring forth this mud-coloured child?'

But no, even if he knew that his father hadn't been entirely right. It wasn't that the cultural gaps were too big; it was just that their colours were so glaringly different. That and nothing else was the terrible crime, the unforgivable sin — this fusion of two colours into one. It was merely a matter of colour, he knew — nothing else. It didn't matter any more what you were, or who you were, or what you thought, or how you felt — all that had ceased to matter, only your colour mattered. Even before you had said one word, the colour of your skin had spoken already and it had spoken loudly; it had spoken even when you were still far away in the distance, to establish what would seem to be the truth about you, the whole truth and nothing but the truth.

Just then John saw a tall, tired looking Indian doctor walking towards them. Before the doctor could reach the bed, he rushed over and stopped him.

'Well, has she got up?' he asked with a cold impersonal stare and a business-like smile.

'No . . . no, I've been waiting.'

The doctor nodded.

'Doctor,' he said hesitating for a while. He was afraid the doctor would soon move away.

'Doctor, I'm worried . . . She's pregnant; is the child all right?'

The doctor had obviously expected the question, 'Well,' he said, 'I checked up on that right away. There has definitely been a lot of shock . . . ' And he stopped as if that was the final verdict.

27

Somehow he knew the doctor wasn't being frank — he seemed to be uneasy about something.

'Please doctor, tell me the truth . . . '

'Well the truth is, we don't know yet. There is a fifty per cent chance, either it'll be born perfectly all right . . . or . . . or it won't. But you see we can't be sure right now.'

He stared blankly at the doctor for a while.

'But if it isn't all right, will it be dead already?'

The doctor nodded gravely.

'You mustn't get worried though,' the doctor reassured him. 'If it's dead, it'll be born dead but it won't be complicated. On the other hand, if we're lucky, it'll be born perfect.'

Then he stopped. Somehow he could feel that his baby wasn't going to be born perfect. It would be born dead already. He could feel it — it was as if the terrible news was written all over the place.

He stared steadily at the doctor. It seemed to be written there too. He stared at him still. It was the look of a condemned man — the look of a man who would suffer bravely and bitterly because the crime was not his and yet the nature of the matter was such that there was nothing else he could do save suffer in silence.

'You aren't going to tell her, are you?' he asked finally.

'No, the shock'll be too much. She'd better not know it. It'll be better that way.' He nodded slowly. For a moment there was tense silence. The doctor must have felt sorry at his distress. He placed his hand on the man's shoulder and said, 'I'm sorry.'

He looked at the doctor blankly and bit his lips. You couldn't, he thought, you couldn't possibly. You didn't love her, you didn't even know her. Why *should* you feel sorry?

'Thank you,' he murmured still biting his lips. The doctor had already walked away.

So there it is, he thought. The cultural gap that had been compromised. The colour gap. Death of a baby in the womb. Like a rosebud plucked away and denied the beauty of the petals.

It was a long while — a painfully long while before she opened her

28

eyes. He sat by her bedside, his hands holding the sides of her neck as if it were a cup. He stared into her eyes. His own face was distorted.

Strangely, he felt helpless and angry at the same time. He wanted to cry and tell her they had hurt his soul and mind more than they had hurt her body. You have cried, he wanted to say, because they made you bleed and they hurt your body. Soon the hurt will have heeled and you won't feel so bad. But what about me, he wanted to ask her. They haven't hurt me, I haven't lost any blood and yet it's my soul and mind that they have turned into pulp. I feel a coward. I wish I had never known you for you must hate me now.

But what did one say? And again he felt guilty. How did one apologise for his race? Did one say: I'm sorry I'm black. I'm sorry you're white?

Then he felt a strange and acute bitterness; he seemed so inadequate, suffocated, and could not help her. He couldn't tell her that the baby wasn't safe any more.

She was staring at him, waiting for him to say something.

He felt her hands touch his as she shook her head slowly.

There was a group of young Africans — probably students, standing a little distance away from his car. As he walked towards his car, with his friend, one of the students said,

'Shucks! We taught them a thing or two, these whites!'

'Yeah,' the other replied. 'Do you know what? . . . There was a white woman standing near the Christos and she laughed at us. She *actually* laughed! Well one of our boys slapped her right over the face . . . It was a direct hit, you read in the papers about the Americans doing it in North Vietnam . . . By God, she actually laughed!'

He started the engine and began getting the car out from between the two cars that were parked in front and at the back. Two of the students came over and started directing him. Finally when he was able to get the car out with their help, he neither looked at them nor thanked them. Full of fury, he drove off at full speed.

While he was still within earshot, one of the boys said, 'Black bastard. Because he's got a Mercedes, he needn't thank us. Except for the colour of their skins, some of our swines aren't any different from the whites . . .'

OMEN

A naked Son — a yellow Sun
A Sun all naked at early dawn
Pours waves of gold over the bank
Of the river of yellow.

A naked Son — a white Sun
A Sun all naked and white
Pours waves of silver
Over the river of white.

A naked Son — a red Sun
A Sun all naked and red
Pours waves of blood
Over the river of red.

Yasmin Jaffer   (15)

THE TROUBADOUR OF CAMELOT

Madanjeet Singh Sandhu

Brown butterfly
You sipped fable-orchids of Enchanted Wood:
Your gossamer wings perturbed
The musked atmosphere with tremulous fright;
Musked with the scent of blood.

Vain flutterfly
You teased the trolls and dryads
To admire your foreign beauty
And stood
In careless vulnerability.

And your fingers were delicate:
They plucked
(No! No! Oh harsh, oh crude
Word
To convey that feathery touch,
Soft-soft breath of water-babies
Napping on the shores of faery glades)
Silver arpeggios on the seven-coloured
Baliset of gods —
'Twas not for you, the instrument
Curving in the drizzle

Across lonely beaches and sylvan groves —
But you
Stealer of nectar
Stole the sacred melody of happiness
And sang it
To your children
Who sat, faces smudged with wild honey and dew

But you woke them up.

Fatuous gutterfly
Sip now the flowers of concrete orchards —
Jangle the copper strings
That stretch from pylon to pylon,
And sing desperate snatches
Of forlorn songs, to asphalt —
Until you wake them up.

THE CAMP

From Uganda, I came to England by air. The journey was noisy and sad. From the airport, we went straight to the camp. It was a long journey. I sat and looked out of the window and thought of home. When we arrived at the camp, they asked us a lot of questions. I couldn't understand why they were asking such a lot of questions. After a long time they showed us our room. It was better then, and we slept there.

The next day, in the morning, we went to have our breakfast. After breakfast we went for a walk in the park. It was a lovely day and we made some English friends. That was nice for I wasn't so lonely anymore.

One day, when we were going for a walk, an English lady came and said, "Come with me, you are going to have a coat." We went to a room. There was a play room as well. We went to play in the play room and met a teacher. He played with us.

The lady told us to come again the next day. We were a lot of children and the lady liked playing rounders very much. I scored many points for our team. One day a man came and reported to my father that he must send us to school. So my sister and I started going to School. We liked going to school. Oursir was an English man. He was just like Mr Mukherjee. I was in school for three weeks. I liked that school very much.

Every Sunday coaches came to take people to London. Some of them wanted to come to Southall. My aunt lives in Southall. I do not like to come to Southall, but my father said, "You have to come." When we came to Southall, I did not like it. My father and my mother and I went back to the camp. When we got back to the camp, my father thought of going to Scotland. But my mother said, "No, we don't want to go to Scotland. It is very cold there." So we didn't go to Scotland and we came to Southall.

Hansa Patel (12)

FROM CITIZEN TO REFUGEE
Extracts from the novel by Mahmood Mamdani

ARRIVAL

'Are you sure it is ten in the morning? It looks more like six in the evening.'

'Oh yes, it is ten. Just you wait. You'll soon learn to talk about the weather first thing in the morning.'

We had disembarked at Heathrow. Having passed through London some years ago as a student, I thought I would share my experience of English weather with my fellow passengers. We walked up a long hallway, clean, almost clinical, like a stretched-out hospital corridor.

'Your vaccination certificate please.' Queuing had by now become a reflex action with us. So we queued as we tried to hold on to our pieces of luggage and fumble through our papers to get out the health certificates.

With the health formalities over, another corridor led us into the main immigration room. There were three queues: British, Commonwealth and Irish, and All Other Nationals. I confidently walked over to the official on the British desk and handed him my passport.

'Sorry, you must queue in the Commonwealth section.'

'But we are British.'

'Yes I know.'

'So things still haven't changed,' I hissed under my breath.

Asians with British passports had had to join the Commonwealth queue before, and apparently now as well. But, as it turned out, the Uganda Resettlement Board had its people at the Commonwealth section, eight of them, an Indian, an American, two Canadians and the rest English. The English volunteers, except for one, were all women. This would become an established pattern in the camps. The volunteers were always women. English men inevitably represented officialdom.

We sat around waiting to be individually cleared. Three older women, wearing what looked like green girl guide uniforms, took turns serving coffee or tea with biscuits. For children, there was orange drink. The processing took little time. My turn came round quickly.

'Yes, young man, do you know anyone in England?'

'Yes, my parents are in a camp. Could I please join them?'

'Let me see . . . Yes . . . it's Kensington Student Centre. They have no doctor there. Would you please step aside so we can X-ray you?'

Another ten minutes and the X-ray was over. Clearly, the staff here was experienced and efficient. In the meantime, an older Asian lady had joined me. She was also to be taken to Kensington, but her luggage had been misplaced. She spoke but a few words of English.

'Please don't leave me. I know I am old and slow, and a burden on a young man like you. But please, stay with me until we get to the camp.'

'Certainly.' I said. But she was not convinced. Every few minutes, while we looked for and finally found her luggage, she kept on repeating the same request; each time it sounded more like a desperate plea. I was very tired, and gradually sympathy gave way to irritation.

What we had expected to be a few minutes interruption in this efficient process was turning out to be a tedious four hour wait, while they decided on a mode of transportation for us. I talked to the lady for a while and then tried to read a little. The volunteers stood in a corner talking to each other; we sat in another corner keeping to ourselves. The Indian volunteer must have realized that we were both tired and restless; he crossed over and tried to talk a little of Uganda.

'You want to go to Kensington? Would you please follow me?' I realized the English volunteer was talking to me.

'We'll take a taxi,' he said. Great, soon I'll be in the camp! Between the two of us there were three suitcases, four handbags and a sitar.

'Anything to declare?' the customs official stopped us. The volunteer gave me an inquiring look. Surely, there must have been a mistake, I thought.

'We have just come from Uganda and brought along whatever we could of our possessions. Surely, you are not going to charge us customs duty?'

'I am afraid you must declare goods like anybody else coming into this country. And if there is customs duty to be paid, you must pay it.'

'But isn't there any exemption for Asians from Uganda?'

'No sir, I am sorry. Nobody is entitled to special treatment.'

Special treatment? Don't special circumstances *demand* special treatment? I felt I was entering an alien world. Carefully, the official went through our luggage. Fortunately, there was nothing that should have been declared.

Once outside, the volunteer looked for a taxi.

'I'm sorry, there seems to be no taxi. Shall we take a bus?' Was he asking my opinion, or politely informing me of the next course of action? It was the latter.

We got into the bus, and then into another, switching to a tube, and finally to a third bus. Every time I got on or off the bus I managed to bang my sitar against a railing. I wondered if I had cracked it. 'Oh, what did it matter,' I thought.

The volunteer was a man of few words. With not even a hello, the conversation was kept down to a few instructional sentences that he uttered at the end or beginning of every ride. I realized he was becoming somewhat uneasy and embarrassed as numerous passengers gave us hostile, or certainly unfriendly glances. A little boy asked his mother:

'Mother, who are they?'

'They are refugees, darling.'

'What's he carrying, Mother?'

'It's an *Indian* instrument, darling. Now why don't you be quiet, dear.'

Finally, we got off the bus and walked into the camp, a large sturdy brick structure. Another volunteer took over.

'Ah yes. You go to Room 44. And get your linen along the way. Just a minute, I'll show you where to get it.'

Room 44 seemed to be thirty feet by ten feet with eight beds arranged in hospital fashion. Four beds were already occupied, and the fifth was mine. Gradually the four occupants came in, one after another. They had all arrived either just a few hours or days before me. For the next two and a half months we would live together in the same room.

* * * *

That first evening, after dinner, we ventured to the camp gate, which opened on to Kensington Church Street. It was about nine in the evening, and we stood there looking at the people passing by. One group, two couples and an older lady, stopped and asked if we were Uganda Asians.

'*Uganda* Asians? Of course, yes we are,' it struck me that in the past three months in Uganda we had been collectively referred to as the *British* Asians; now in Britain, we would be called *Uganda* Asians. They started talking, were slightly tipsy, but very nice. One of them was paraphrasing the rather mixed welcome message the *Economist* had put on its cover the month before.

'We know we didn't always want you here, and we know you didn't really want to come, but now that you are here, we are glad. Let's learn to live together.'

'But we *did* want to come,' one of the group broke in. The conversation shifted to Amin.

'He's really a Julius Caesar, isn't he?'

'Yes, it's a shame there is no Brutus.'

The older woman looked up, a little startled. 'My they are civilized, aren't they? Listen to the English they speak.'

'If we were in France, *they* wouldn't think we were civilized because we spoke good English.'

That stopped things a little. We all realized there was no need for bitterness, so the topic was changed. We talked amiably for another ten minutes and then went our separate ways.

The next morning, after breakfast, we were back at the gate. On the other side of the street a number of people stood in a bus queue, most of them reading a morning paper.

'Something important has happened, perhaps in Uganda. Let's get a paper,' somebody suggested. Gradually, sometimes amusingly, but not always so, we were learning of English habits.

That evening we ventured out of the gate again, this time going a bit further down Church Street and along the busy looking street at the corner. It was Kensington High Street: Barker's, Derry and Tom's, Woolworths . . .

'This is like twenty Draper's (the largest clothing store in Kampala) put into one,' Ben remarked, as he peered into Derry and Tom's.

'Yes, it's like all of Kampala put into one street,' S.S. agreed.

We had read of the English as being a nation of shopkeepers. This seemed more like a nation of shoppers. We walked around, gradually, looking at the window displays, reading advertisements, translating pounds into Uganda shillings; generally absorbed by all the things around us. The people were rushing by at too quick a pace to be examined individually. At the tube station, however, there were two long queues, one in front of a bus stop, another at the newspaper stand.

'Look at the women. Incredible!' Yes, they were quite incredible or rather, strange. Like a parade of exotic creatures in a national game park: every shade of cosmetic one could have imagined; hair from jet black to colourless stringy blonde; their faces set with definite expressions; life on stage.

'Look at her, she must have been a zebra in her previous life.'

'But look behind her, that's definitely a gazelle.'

The gazelle represented a different breed, definitely a minority, not so obviously made up, very much the product of what must have been a most delicate and complex process, sans colour, sans taste, sans odour; ethereal, like air.

'It must be hard work to be a woman in this place. I don't think I would like it,' Patel summed up our feelings.

In the next few days, however, we realized that it wasn't such a nice feeling to walk up and down Kensington High Street among people who seemed to be buying things just about all the time. Our resources were limited to social security payments of £2.10 a week. With such a meagre income, buying anything was out of the question. But all around us was incessant consumption, staring at us from every window were things just waiting to be bought, to be eaten, to be worn, to be read. Large and small signs, they all urged one to acquire and made one feel deprived, however temporary the feeling may be.

One of the signs read: 'Don't you need a new coat this winter?' Of course, we needed it. But our demand was not what the economist calls 'effective demand.' In the market place, where the demand curve meets the supply curve, we had no resources to represent our needs. Under such circumstances, looking at life on Kensington High Street seemed like seeing the city through its ass-hole.

Gradually, we began to acquire habits that people usually associated with the lower classes; in Uganda, with the African domestic servants. Every Friday, we received our £2.10 social security. By Sunday, it was all gone, on cigarettes and drinks. All the money, however, was very little money. It didn't take many weeks to realize that saving makes sense only to those whose incomes are above a certain level. To those who have very little to begin with, there is little incentive to save. One's position in the social hierachy, and its vast influence on the shaping of individual or group life, was gradually becoming clear to us.

* * * *

40

THE CAMP

'You're cold. Why don't you go downstairs and get a warm sweater and a coat. It's free. There's a women's voluntary organization which hands it out. Come, I'll show you where it is.' Ben led me downstairs, to the WRVS clothing room.

'You are . . . '

'Mamdani.'

'O.K. Mr Mamdani. I have got a coat just for you. It's a Parisian cape. Only slightly worn. Not more than two years old. And a hat to go with it. My, it's from Harrods too.' She examined the hat, and then added, 'Harrods — that's where the rich in this country do their shopping.'

Fitted in my Parisian cape and a Harrods' bowler hat, with wire-rimmed glasses, a bushy moustache, and curly black hair coming out from under the black hat, I must have looked quite ridiculous. As I strolled out into the car park that fills the space between the two large concrete buildings that were the camp, the young Nigerian car attendant looked me up and down:

'Hey man, what you need is an umbrella,' he broke out into peals of laughter.

Standing next to me was a smartly-dressed middle-aged lady, waiting to pay her parking fee. Trying hard to conceal the smile on her face, she turned to her dog, a well-groomed white poodle that she led by a chain. I followed her gaze; heavens! even the dog was clothed! There seemed a curious similarity between the poodle and me: both dressed in the ways of an alien world. For a few seconds, the car attendant and the lady seemed to share this realization — and they laughed freely. The next moment, however, the lady seemed embarassed and apologetic; she hurried through the ticket payment and hastily walked to her car. The Nigerian just shook his head,

'The Man's got you, boy.' I wondered whatever he meant, if anything at all.

What I couldn't miss was the fact that there was something wrong with the cape-hat-Asian combination. Once back in the room, I discarded the bowler hat.

* * * *

A QUESTION OF IDENTITY
'General Amin has nationalised British plantations in Uganda,' the word spread through the camp. At news time, the canteen was crowded. After explaining the substance of the General's latest decree and the nature of British interests affected, the BBC reporter proceeded to question the new African manager of a formerly British-owned tea plantation:

'The General maintains that Uganda doesn't need the British. If so, why weren't these plantations developed before the British arrived here? What were you doing then?'

The television interview ended. But the reporter's question was answered by one of the people in the canteen: 'They were on trees then.' It was the most extreme racial utterance I had heard from one of my compatriots. It was not simply the racial view of the world a person born and bred in colonial Uganda inherited. Amin's own brutal racialism had intensified this racial consciousness. Put simply, the majority of Uganda Asians who came to Britain had become racialists through experience. The very first day I was in the camp, I remember Shivji, one of the people on my floor, saying, 'Africans are unfit to rule. Perhaps the British should never have left Uganda.'

Sad, and yet angry, I retorted: 'Have you ever heard of what happened during the Indian partition, of what the Pakistanis did in Bangla Desh, or the British in Ireland? Tell me, are Asians "fit to rule" in your terms?'

He shrugged his shoulders. I realized that an argument, no matter how persuasive in the abstract, would take us nowhere. But in the coming weeks it became clear that Shivji, among others, was in for another set of experiences, one that would shatter his view of the

42

world.

In the next few weeks Shivji was one of the few people who started leaving the camp to see London and to find himself a job. Gradually he learned to travel by tube. At first, he noticed the inevitable writing on the wall: 'wogs out'. Once in a while he would realize that the tube was fairly crowded but the seat next to him conspicuously empty. And after a few days, he learned that if you are coloured and are lost in a tube station it is better to approach a West Indian guard rather than his white counterpart. Every evening he would tell us about his experiences when we gathered after dinner. 'Some West Indians are really nice, aren't they?' he once remarked a little sheepishly.

That week two Asian youths came to visit the camps. They had been born in Britain and wanted to know how the 'brothers' were doing. The conversation centred on the British: in Uganda and in Britain. Everybody was enjoying exchanging experiences. The common theme was the nastiness of the British. At this point, one of our visitors remarked:

'Yes, we blacks must unite and defend ourselves.'

'We blacks? What does he mean?' Patel turned to me.

'Yes, *we*. I mean nobody is really black. We are all different shades of brown. They call us coloured. We should call ourselves black and fight for Black Power.'

'Black Power?'

'Yes, look, we are from a group called Black Liberation Front. All black people should unite in self-defence against the white power structure.'

Incredulous, Patel laughed: 'Are you crazy? I am not black. Nobody here is black. We are neither white nor black. We are brown.'

The visitor persisted: 'You don't understand . . . ' The next half hour was quite bizarre. Like two lanes on a motorway, running parallel to one another, but with the traffic going in opposite directions, not meeting at any point. During the evening get-together there were some remarks about our visitors from Shivji. 'I can believe that West

Indians are nice people. But that we are all black! Phew!'

A few days later, Shivji received a letter from a friend who lived about fifty miles to the north.

'He is asking me to go and visit him. He says he can find me a job and I can stay with him. I'll be back in two days. Patel, why don't you come with me? The Board's not going to do anything for us, you know that. You will simply sit and rot.'

'I'll come. Why not. I have nothing else to do.'

The day after, Shivji and Patel returned.

'Well, did you find a job?'

'Yes. But I don't know if I am going to take it. I think I want to live in a place where there are a number of *our* people.'

'What are you talking about?'

'Patel, you explain it.'

Patel sat down, his legs crossed in a yoga position, as if ready to tell a long story:

'Well, you see, it was like this. Tuesday night, Shivji and I were walking around in this place. All by ourselves. I don't know what the English call the town. Anyway, we met four whites on the streets. One of them turned to Shivji and said, "Hey blackie, what are you doing here? Why don't you go home?" Imagine, they called us *blackie;* not even *coloured.* We ignored them, but they came to us and this one said: "We'll teach you a lesson. We are going to beat you up." Four against the two of us. Some of these whites are tough. I started saying my prayers. Just then, as if God had answered, there came four West Indians. I think they had been following us and had listened to everything. One of them said to Shivji, "Don't worry, brother. We'll take care of them." But the whites had run away. And you know what this West Indian said? He didn't even ask our names; he simply said:

' "Look here, brother, it may have been different in Africa. But here, we are all brothers. For the white man, we are all black. So, forget this coloured shit." '

Shivji, who had been listening to Patel's account of the episode, added :

'Yes, Patel has said it. That's what happened. Maybe those liberation people have something to say. I don't care about the Board. *I* am going to live in a Red Area.' (According to the lingo of the Board, a Red Area is where there are 'too many coloureds.')

Shivji had learned that the definition of race is *social*. In Uganda, we were Asians, and that meant being not-white and not-black. But here in England, we were simply not-white.

But there were others who differed from Shivji, who *did not* want to live in Red Areas. One week-end, Jagdish, my old friend from Kampala, came to visit us. He had gone to Bristol, determined to re-settle himself. In the evening, I introduced him to people on my floor. Patel made coffee and we sat and talked.

At that point Jamal came in. He lived next door with his parents. His father had been affluent in Kampala, and had had an overseas bank account in Switzerland. They were in the camp 'for a few weeks while we look for a house.'

'Listen to the good news. We have found a house. Tomorrow we sign the papers.'

'Where is it?'

'Near Cockfosters. You probably haven't heard of the area. That's where a lot of rich English people live. There are no Asians there. It's a really good area.'

'What's good about there being no Asians there?'

'You don't understand. It's an upper class area. In an area with a lot of Asians, the property values go down. No English people want to live in such an area.'

When Jamal left, Jagdish remarked :

'Hm. A good area because there are no Asians there. What can one call it but self-hatred. Doesn't he realize he is an Asian? When he moves in, the whites will start leaving, and he'll be left there all by himself, with nothing but declining property values and other rich Asians moving in because "it is a good area".'

'Don't worry, Jagga. Jamal will learn.'

45

'I just wish everybody didn't have to *learn*. By the time we all learn we may be dead.'

* * * *

UGANDA

I would like to write about Uganda.

Uganda is the best country I've ever seen. I liked it there very much. It is a dry country. The people who live there are black and are called Africans. I was born there.

We had a very big house and a timber yard. We had five rooms in our house. I went to a school called the pioneer school. It was very nice and there were many African teachers there. We used to learn Maths, English, History, Geography, Science and Civics.

In Uganda there were many parks. The biggest park was Murchison Park. It was a park and a falls. There were many big towns in Uganda. We lived near Kampala, but not very near, about two hundred miles away. We had a very nice garden there. We had a fluffy dog.

The Africans are very good. They do everyone's work and earn money. When my sister was small our servant used to take her to the park and teach her how to catch balls and how to kick a ball. The African people are always very clean. Sometimes we used to play with them. We had rounders, netball and many things to play. Sometimes we raced to see who won. So it was very good. Sometimes the Africans brought mangos and many fruits. If we gave them one shilling they gave us fresh fruits. We went to play at four o'clock and we came home at six o'clock. Then we used to go back to the park and play until seven or half-past seven. There were many big animals which we could see in Uganda.

But now the African people will not get their food or money. I think they will cry. When we came here they were crying very much.

Here all the people work in the factories, but there if only one person worked the whole family would eat. Here all the people are white. There all the people are black. There was a European club and we used to go there to swim everyday. And on Friday we ate our dinner there; we had fish and chips. Everyday we went to the club to drink Coca-Cola and eat crisps. Our servant came with us and played with my sister.

They gave us books from the school but we had to take our own pens. On Saturday and Sunday we went swimming alone. Sometimes the beggars came to our home for money and food.

Dipti Patel (10)

KONGI'S HARVEST
Jagjit Singh

Tyranny has an evil face
and no particular colour,
and so my brethren, black and brown
do not go gentle into that foreign land,
rage, rage against the savagery of this slaughter.

And I shall mourn also
death of those that dared to dissent,
victims of gun-point disappearances,
innocents caught in cross-fires
and of soldiers too, blown to bits
for being born of the wrong tribe.

And the Nile
restless final resting place for the massacred,
is made a silent accomplice —
bodies now littered for alligators
will soon be washed in deep down gulfs of liquid fire
for the Nile
is become a quick, cold painful grave,
and quiet flows the blood
of many thousands gone.

I shall proclaim my brotherhood therefore
with all those that have died,
that have suffered —

be it in apartheid's sordid cells
where Letters to Martha were written,
or the cold Siberian snows
where sufferings of the innocent
are evidence of cancer wards,
or the gaols of recent civil wars
where too the man died,
and nearby battlefields
scene where madmen and specialists changed roles
and earth's lips were congealed with blood.

Let me say it then,
voice raging aloud:

Divided though we may have been
by race and history
in suffering are we become one
with the Lombeys and Lawinos, Ocols and the Orphans —
backs broken, black-brown broken,
mere shadows of our former selves,
exiled to silence if not massacred outrageously . . .

For tyranny has an evil face
and no particular colour:
do not therefore go gentle into that foreign land,
rage, rage against the savagery of this slaughter.

MYSELF

I am a girl. My name is Shushma. Do you think it's a pretty name sir? I am eleven years old. My birthday is on April 18th. I used to live in Uganda, in a town called Masindi. The name of my school was Masindi Public School.

My father was an accountant, and my mother was a housewife. My eldest brother was trying to come to London, after finishing his 'O' levels. He wants to go to Cambridge. My brother Dilesh and I were at school.

On August 4, 1972, the President of Uganda announced that people holding British passports, Bangladesh passports, Pakistani passports and Indian passports should be out of the country within a time of three months, that is November 7, 1972.

So, all the people holding those passports started getting their documents ready. People had a lot of trouble just because of the cruel Africans of Uganda beating, killing and taking people away.

My father started getting all the documents ready. As my father was working in a government department, we could not come here early. After a lot of trouble, everything was ready and we came here on October 10th. We landed at Heathrow Airport, from there we were taken, first on a bus, then on a train, to a camp in Wales, called Tonfanafu.

In the camp I had many friends and we enjoyed ourselves. I used to go to school. I was put in form two. The name of our teacher was Mrs Muir and the headmaster was Mr Jones. There were three schools and a play centre. The schools were for Infants, Juniors and Seniors.

We used to go to the canteen to eat and have our breakfast. Some houses had everything and there were also some flats. We used to stay in one of those flats.

At the end, it was announced that the camp was going to be

closed, so my father started looking for a house in London. Soon we had a letter from my uncle, living in Hayes. He wrote that there was a house in Southall, so we came to stay over there.

I like the weather and the school. It's not as cold here as it was in Wales.

That's all about myself.

Shushma Patel (12)

MY FRIEND

I had a friend in Kampala. He was a very kind boy. If my little brother asked him for a ball, he gave it to him forever. His name was Nalin. He was eleven years old. He was a year younger than me. He never fought with me. It is a pity that he wasn't very good at his lessons.

We used to play football, hockey and badminton. During the holidays we played cricket. I used to live with him during the holidays. We both used to laugh a lot. He was very funny and made me laugh. We used to go to school together at 7.30 a.m. and come back in the afternoon for lunch, and go back again.

After school we played. We enjoyed playing cricket, which was our favourite sport. Sometimes I went to his house and sometimes he came to mine. When I came to England, he was very unhappy, and so was I. I often think of the big tree near our house. We used to sit under the tree and talk to each other. When our friends came, we made up a team and played cricket. Now, whenever I see a big tree, I think of Nalin. I like playing but now I don't have anyone to play with. It is sad. Now, in the evenings I sit and watch television. I think of him and I am sure he thinks of me. I will remember him forever.

Virji Singdia (12)

53

SWEET SCUM OF FREEDOM
Extracts from the radio play by Jagjit Singh

List of characters:

KEVAL: Young Asian student, 21 years old, is flying off to England the next day to study medicine. Nervous, romantic, sentimental, sexually inexperienced.

ANNA: African prostitute, 28 years old, mature and understanding. Motherly attitude towards Keval. Has a kind voice and baby twins. Normally speaks good English but lapses into bad grammar when excited.

TWINS: About nine months old. Cry occasionally during the play.

DR EBONGO: African politician/businessman, 50 years old. A very deep and arrogant voice. Fiercely anti-West during colonial days but a fat, comfortable minister now. Director of several companies but also a committed 'African Socialist'. A strong critic of the Asians and of prostitution.

THE VOICE: Radio newsreader, 30 years old. African accent but not as deep as Ebongo. Not very coherent.

Time: The present.

Place: A newly independent country with a small Asian and European population. Member of the Commonwealth, OAU, UNO, etc., etc.

Keval is flying off to England the following day. He visits Anna, the African prostitute, for the last time. She tells him the latest news — that Dr Ebongo, the minister, has been stabbed by a prostitute at the Lorina night club. Keval does not particularly admire Dr Ebongo. He is talking to Anna. They have just finished making love.

KEVAL: I will miss you Anna.

ANNA: Why? How do you mean?

KEVAL: I'm going away tomorrow.

ANNA: Eeeeee! Going away? **Where?**

KEVAL: I'm going away to England tomorrow.

ANNA: Eeeeee! To England? But your father is a citizen. Why you want to go?

KEVAL: Yes. Yes, my father is a citizen. Third class citizen!
(LAUGHS)   He's also got the trade licence. But I'm still going to England.

ANNA: But why you go? You not citizen yourself then?

KEVAL: (PAUSE. THEN LAUGHS AGAIN) I don't know. Don't even care. Three times I've applied. Three times they've cancelled it. Dr Ebongo and the government can't decide! So I can't go to our own university. Even if they let me go there, they won't let me do Law, or Commerce, or Medicine. First preference to Africans because Asians are parasites. Parasites will only be allowed to do B.A. in History or English. How can I help my father with History?

56

(PAUSE) So I'm going to study in England.

ANNA: What will you study?

KEVAL: Well, actually I want to be a writer. I'll write stories
               and plays and longer short stories called novels.
               But I'll be very poor because there's no money in it
               and also it is a lot of hard work. You have to study
               all the big words in the English dictionary. . . Any-
               way my father wants me to be a doctor or an
               engineer because then I can be very rich. So I'll
               become a doctor.

               (FAINT SOUNDS OF DOGS BARKING OUT-
               SIDE)

ANNA: What will you write in your stories, Keval?

KEVAL: (SIGHS) About you.
               And about the wretchedness of being an Indian in
               Africa today. Always being the brown man out, the
               odd man, the foreigner, the wahindi. . . Little
               frightened fishes swimming frantically in water
               made dirty by our own commerce and trade; al-
               ways afraid the big black minister will pull us out
               of the fishing pond and throw us away, far, far
               away and we will die without our commerce and
               trade. Yes, I'll write about how frightened and
               wretched we are today — always being bullied and
               insulted everywhere — in parliament, on the radio,
               on TV, on the roads and even here by a bitch like
               Sunma who called me a parasite and spit on my
               face. (PAUSE) Yes, I'll write about all this. Because
               it isn't our fault only. The British brought us here

to trade and build railways because Africans couldn't do it. Dirt carriers we were of the British. . . and dirt carriers we shall remain. No, it wasn't our fault. . . . It's only that we've become such cowards these days. . . (PAUSE)

ANNA: Is the same with us also, I tell you. I don't like our ministers. They promise us many things before Uhuru. Uhuru comes. We get nothing; the ministers take everything for themselves. Is the same with all rich men. I don't like them.

(TWINS CRY AGAIN. SITAR MUSIC COMES TO AN END. HOWLING WINDS HIT ON THE DOOR. SHE GETS UP TO GO TO THE TWINS)

KEVAL: How are they — the twins?

ANNA: Same as always. When they're big I'll send them to government school. Same school where you go! Ramgolam says he will give me money for the fee.

KEVAL: If Ramgolam is still around! Government doesn't like Asian shopkeepers. Africanisation! They might kick him in the arse. He might have to go to India.

ANNA: No. Ramgolam is African citizen. He has passport. Also trade licence. So he stay.

KEVAL: (LAUGHS) O.K. so he stay. He give you money to send them school. Then I come back. I be their doctor. I give them free injection. Huh? Good. No?

58

ANNA: I don't know.
(MURMURS TO THE TWINS TO STOP CRY-
ING. HE GETS UP)

* * * *

(FADE ON TO NEWS)

VOICE: And we return once again to the most important
headlines for the day. The condition of Dr Ebongo,
our minister of Commerce and Trade, Broadcast-
ing, Foreign and Cultural affairs continues to be
critical. He has had an emergency operation. Dr
Ebongo was stabbed twice in the chest, by a woman
of low character at the Lorina night club where he
was relaxing after a hard day in parliament. The
woman and six others were immediately arrested.
Dr Ebongo was to fly tomorrow to New York to
speak in the United Nations Security Council
special debate on Russia. . . . I beg your pardon, on
Rhodesia. The Prime Minister, Dr Ingola, has expressed utter shock, surprise and bewilderment at
this callous and most cruel crime. To injure a man
of Dr Ebongo's calibre, gallant and patriotic freedom fighter, is a national calamity and a crime
against humanity, Dr Ingola has said. The Prime
Minister has himself cut short his visit to Addis
Ababa where he was speaking on the OAU emergency debate on Rhodesia. Dr Ingola will be flying
home tomorrow.
Meanwhile the Minister of Defence and Internal
Affairs has declared a state of emergency and the

army has been put on the alert. All political activities and parties have been banned. The leader of the opposition, Mr Kapu Iyololo, has been detained under the Emergency Powers. . .

KEVAL: Good God, so it's a short cut to a one party state.

ANNA: Sssssh. Listen to the news.

VOICE: Meanwhile messages of sympathy have been coming in from all over the world. The American, French and Russian Ambassadors, the Canadian and Indian High Commissioners and the British Charge D'Affaires have already called on Mrs Ebongo to pay their respects. . .

KEVAL: Wow! So it's VIP treatment, huh?

ANNA: Ssssh. Listen. . .

VOICE: Dr Ebongo also launched a passionate attack on prostitution in parliament today. Referring to them as the scum that is today disgracing the heroic freedom struggle of our people, he went on to quote Chairman Mao on the best way of wiping out this disgraceful disease. It is reported a number of prostitutes have already been arrested following this evening's shocking attempt on the life of Dr Ebongo by a woman of low character. Police will carry out a house to house search in the Wandegya area.

ANNA: Eeeeee! They will arrest us. They will come here. What'll I do?

KEVAL: Sssssssh! Listen to the news.

VOICE: And now we broadcast an extract from Dr Ebongo's speech on the Asian Community. . .

DR EBONGO'S
VOICE: Mr Chairman, Ladies and Gentlemen, it is a very, very well known fact that the African has always been exploited. Under the dedicated leadership of our Prime Minister, Dr Ingola, we have finally pushed the British Imperialists out of our beautiful land. Africa is now free — Uhuru na Africa! Today, Ladies and Gentlemen, Africa is free — that is to say except Rhodesia, Angola, Mozambique and South Africa which no doubt our brothers will soon liberate. But the African is still very, very oppressed, I tell you — economically oppressed! We still have a lot of foreigners in our country. I am referring of course to the Asian Community. They have done a good job in the past but I must regret the winds have changed now.

I ask my Asian brothers and sisters: How many of you fought side by side with your African brothers when we were involved in a life and death struggle with British colonialism? How many I ask you? How many of you suffered and died with the Africans during the freedom struggle? And I ask you Ladies and Gentlemen: How many of you have become our citizens today? We believe in the United Nations Human Rights Charter and we ask the Asians to join us wholeheartedly in the great struggle against humanity's common enemies — poverty, disease and hunger. But I must warn the Asians. We will never allow them to have one foot in Britain, the other foot in India and only their hands in Africa, playing like prostitutes with our Commerce and Trade. We will never allow any money to be sent out of the country. The best answer is to become our citizens, live with us, work with us, eat with us, even marry us. Yes, I tell you, inter-racial marriage is the only answer to this problem. And so, Mr Chairman, Ladies and Gentlemen, in conclusion, allow me merely to add that. . .

(FADE OFF)

KEVAL: (VERY QUIETLY) Three times I have applied for citizenship. Three times they have turned me down. And now Dr Ebongo says become citizens!

ANNA: But why don't the Asians marry Africans? Why are your people so frightened?

(PAUSE)

KEVAL: (SLOWLY) Yes, I ask myself, why are we so frightened? Why don't we marry Africans and Europeans. . . Oh, I love half-caste children — brown, chocolate brown, mud brown, brick brown, coffee brown, tree bark, dry leaf, wood-love brown, ebony brown with large black eyes, black curly hair — like, like your twins Anna.

ANNA: Yes, like my twins. And like their father Ramgolam, shop-keeper down the road!

KEVAL: (SIGHS) But it will never happen Anna! We are frightened. The Asians are such a frightened people. They're so pure and clean — must say their prayers and wash their bodies every day. And they are so rich — most of them and they have big shops and big cars and you don't. They'll never marry you. Besides, black is so untame and dangerous for them. And they'll always call half-caste children Chotaras.

ANNA: Chotaras? (LAUGHS) So my twins are Chotaras also?

KEVAL: Used to be different when we first came to Africa of course. When we were poor and alone and struggling and without women. Then we slept with African women and had lots of Chotara children. But now we have too much money, too much religion and too many women of our own. And people like Dr Ebongo will never make it any easier for us.

(TWINS START TO CRY)

KEVAL: Give them the doll. (SHE MAKES THE MAA-MAA NOISE WITH THE DOLL A FEW TIMES)

(TWINS STOP CRYING)

KEVAL: Did I tell you about Zeenet, the butcher's daughter who ran off with an African lawyer?

ANNA: No! The butcher? Which one?

KEVAL: (LAUGHS LOUDLY) Yes, the butcher who used

	to come to you last year.
ANNA:	Oooooh, yes. I remember. Why doesn't he come to me anymore?
KEVAL:	Because his daughter ran off and married an African lawyer. That's why!
ANNA:	Eeeee! Really?
KEVAL:	Yes suh! She ran off and married Fred Makonza. She was a secretary at his office. That's how. People say she was a bit of a malaya also, but I don't know. Anyway, Karim Hussein, the father, got so mad, he beat up his wife for not taking proper care of Zeenet. He beat up all his other daughters also and sent them to Pakistan to get married. Poor chap! Then he went around looking for Zeenet himself. Found her at the office and threatened to kill her if she didn't come home with him. But the African lawyer came and pushed him out of the office. You see, Fred Makonza works for the government and he said he would cancel the meat licence or send them a deportation order if Karim Hussein didn't behave himself. Poor Zeenet kept saying 'Papa, please go. Papa, please go.' So Papa finally did go away and beat up his wife even more. So now they're all going back to Pakistan.
ANNA:	(LAUGHS) Eeeee! Is a very good story!
KEVAL:	And they have a little boy now. Zeenet and Fred.
ANNA:	A Chotara boy like the twins?

(SHE LAUGHS WILDLY. HE IS SILENT)
And is your father the same with your sisters?

KEVAL: Oh yes. Kabissa! He's even stopped my sisters from going to the cinema. And no more typing lessons either. Because typists always run away with African lawyers. In fact my father is also sending my sisters to India to get married. Then they can come back.

ANNA: To India?

KEVAL: Yes.

ANNA: Not to England?

KEVAL: No, no, no, no. England is not nice for girls. They get spoilt. They'll only run off with English lawyers there.

ANNA: But what about you?

KEVAL: With boys it is different. (PAUSE)

ANNA: Don't you feel guilty?

KEVAL: What about?

ANNA: About coming to African malayas when your father is so strict with your sisters?

KEVAL: Look here, don't be funny. Understand? Of course I feel guilty. I feel ashamed. But I need you Anna. I need someone. I feel so rotten sneaking into my

65

house at two in the morning, everybody asleep and my mother opening the door, anxiously asking where I've been and I have to lie to her. Always I lie to her. Always I say I was with a friend or something. And she says, bless you child, you mustn't work so hard. And I climb up the stairs, go into the bathroom, wash myself and stare into the mirror. I stare into my hollow eyes and I hate that bastard's face for lying, for being so weak. But what else can I do? I need someone to touch and hold and love and to talk to. Almost anyone. That's why I always come back to you.

ANNA: Yes darling. . . But will you marry me?

KEVAL: Don't be crazy. You know I can't. I'm going to England tomorrow.

*   *   *   *

It is early next morning. Anna turns on the radio. In the background we hear the sound of aeroplane engines. Keval is flying off to England.

VOICE: Good morning, listeners. We now present the early morning six o'clock news. Dr Ebongo's condition continues to be critical. The Prime Minister, Dr Ingola, arrived back from Addis Ababa early this morning and will meet with the cabinet soon to discuss the grave crisis. All political activities and political parties were banned yesterday and a state of emergency has been proclaimed. The Prime Minister has congratulated the Defence and Internal Affairs minister for his prompt and decisive action. No stone must be left unturned in such a grave crisis, he declared. Meanwhile the Prime Minister has personally appealed to the British Government to send more doctors to save the life of Dr Ebongo. When faced with such a calamity, the international community should behave in the true spirit of the United Nations Charter, the Prime Minister declared at the airport. Sources in London say the British Government is expected to react favourably to Dr Ingola's appeal. It is believed the British Government will also take the opportunity to send a Trade and Foreign Aid delegation to discuss long term aid programmes. This will be the first such move by the British Government after our Government broke off diplomatic relations over Rhodesia. The British Charge D'Affaires has already welcomed the move as the beginning of a new era. In parliament yesterday, Dr Ebongo launched a passionate attack against prostitution and referred to them as the scum that is today, disgracing our heroic freedom struggle. Police are still continuing their house search in the Wandegya area and more arrests are likely.

(AEROPLANE ENGINES LOUDER NOW)

In a speech yesterday, Dr Ebongo also appealed to the Asian community to take up citizenship *now* and live and work among the Africans. Inter-racial marriage is the only solution to this. . .
(FADE OFF TO TWINS CRYING, DOLL

SOUND AND *LOUD KNOCKING ON THE DOOR*. PAUSE. *LOUDER KNOCKING*. DEAD SILENCE. *KNOCKING AGAIN.)*

ANNA :   Who. . . who's it? . . .

POLICE :   Open up. . . open up. The police. . .

(KNOCKING)
SILENCE. THEN SHIFT TO AEROPLANE ENGINES — VERY LOUD NOW. AEROPLANE STARTS TO MOVE. POLICEMAN'S VOICE AGAIN. VOICE DROWNED. . .
AEROPLANE TAKES OFF

* * * *

This play was entered for the BBC Radio play for Africa competition and was awarded third prize out of a total of 600 entries by a panel of judges made up of Wole Soyinka, Martin Esslin and Lewis Nkosi.

THE LONELY FOREST

The forest stood still without anything moving
As if time had stopped
The ground was covered with snow
Like a blanket waiting for someone to sleep.

The trees stood still without a move
Like witches waiting for their victim
It was a lonely forest with no other life
Except its own
Without the leaves they looked like dried bones.

The forest waits for spring
To take away the snow and wind
And bring back the birds that used to sing.

Gurdip Chadha (12)

BLACK ON BROWN
Ahmed Virjee

Do not smile and do not laugh,
For they portray your happiness
(While envy and jealousy
Torment me, can't you see?)
So do not smile and do not laugh
On my land.

Do not ruffle the sands of the lake
With your bare feet;
You enjoy the moments of leisure
After toiling in the day;
Do not ruffle the sands
On my land.

Do not dig the fertile soil
And sow your dirty seeds,
For you will reap the harvests
And you will dig the fruits;
So do not dig the soil
Of my land.

Ah, wait! Dig my soil for me,
And sow your clean seeds;
Then reap the harvests for me,
And I will enjoy the fruits;
So dig the soil
Of my land.

Brew as much of the wines
And bake all the bread;
Serve me on a silver platter
While I laze and watch
The blossoming fruits
Of my land.

Give me your lovely women
Richly laden with gold ornaments
And clad in silky garments;
This is all I have wished for,
Then you can stay
On my land.

Build me the tortuous railways
And make me the endless roads
For me to travel and walk on
(After you have quit);
So build for me
On my land.

Make me the palatial houses
And conjure up the Industries
For me to use them;
And teach me all your trades,
And teach me the values
Of my land.

Shatter your cultures;
My culture must stay.
Break away from traditions;
My traditions should remain.
So give me all I want
And then go away
From my land!

NEW ARRIVAL

We came here from Uganda on 8th October, 1972. We had a lot of trouble while coming to Britain. When we arrived here, we were taken to the camp where we stayed for five months. There was no trouble in the camp. It was near the sea-side. The weather was not too bad and every Sunday we used to go to the town.

My father is jobless but he is looking for a job. My mother is also jobless. In Uganda my father was working in the Ministry of Works and Communications as an accountant, and my mother was a housewife. In the camp it was very cold because of the sea, but in Southall it is not cold. I have two other brothers and one sister. Their names are Kaushik, Hiren and Shushma. In Uganda we lived in Masindi. It is a small town.

I am mainly interested in my studies and my brother is taking a course in electronics. My elder brother is in Cambridge this year.

We came from the camp to Southall on 8th February, 1973, then we registered for schools. My father was trying to find a job in the post-office. They have no vacancies. He also tried BEA but he failed the test. We all like Southall. We like the people too, because of their kindness. The buildings are good and the shops are big.

In the camp we used to play football at the weekends. In the holidays we used to go to the sea-side or to the club to play darts, table tennis or watch television. My eldest brother used to go weed-picking near the sea-side and earn money. He used to get £1 for picking four stone. I had many friends in the camp and I have many here.

Dilesh Patel (13)

THE LEADER

Extract from the novel "In a Brown Mantle" by Peter Nazareth

The narrator of the novel is Deo D'Souza, a Goan (Asian) politician from Damibia, East Africa, in self-imposed exile in London.

It was during my second visit to the New Jazz Nightclub, years later, that I met Robert Kyeyune.

My head was buzzing and I decided to take a break and go to the New Jazz Nightclub. If you were from outside Eastern Africa, you would think of the New Jazz Nightclub as just another nightclub, though rather exotic. To a Goan, it was an *African* nightclub carrying with it overtones of the unusual, the underworld, possibly even a tinge of the depraved. It was thought that dances in African nightclubs broke the rules of normal society. Certainly a dance in an African nightclub was totally different from a dance in a Goan Institute.

A dance in a Goan Institute used to be rather formal. The dance usually starts at 9 p.m., which means that the band starts playing around nine-thirty and couples start drifting in at a quarter-to-ten.

The people are semi-formally dressed in attractive dresses or suits. The couples sit on chairs placed around the dance floor or around small tables. If they sit around the dance floor, the men usually vanish to the bar. They then hold their drinks and watch from the side-lines until somebody gathers up the nerve to commence dancing.

Then the men go up to the ladies of their choice (they dance with the wife first) and say, 'May I have the next dance, please?' The reply is usually, 'Yes,' in which case they go around the floor in varying degrees of happiness. (Not Fortunato D'Mello, who never took up dancing. When I asked him why, he said that he one day counted the number of times a couple went round the dance floor.

He then estimated the length and breadth of the floor. After which, he calculated that a couple moved 17 miles round the floor during that dance. 'All that distance and they got nowhere,' he said).

The band plays a set of three pieces — say three quicksteps. Each piece lasts three or four minutes. The band takes a break and the couples return to their seats, the men saying 'Thank you very much' and 'May I get you a drink?'

Then the next dance starts — a set of three foxtrots. And the dancing starts. A break. A set of three rhumbas. Break. Three Shake/Soul. Break. A mild set of African dances. Break.

There is no eroticism in Goan dances. Rather, whatever eroticism exists is submerged and can only be detected when a wolf like Joaquim D'Costa is dancing with a long-married lady. And there is no break in the civilised behaviour, except for the inevitable fight around the bar, which ends by somebody bringing the warring factions together over a drink or by somebody being thrown out.

Go to an African nightclub and you are assailed by electronic wailing before you get in. The guitars send out signals to the neighbouring areas so that all may come to the dance. You pay a couple of shillings at the gate to a brightly painted woman, and enter into a sleazy hall.

The hall is dark and full of music. There is movement everywhere, people dancing or drinking. They are dressed as they like and do what they like. The atmosphere is charged, as though the uninhibited human being is inescapably erotic. Or is it that one is attracted by seeing so many dark, unaccompanied women?

The band plays loudly, deafeningly. You cannot talk because you cannot hear anybody unless he or she shouts. You stand outside, hating the crudeness and vulgarity of it all.

But you start dancing eventually, as you wish, not following any fixed steps. The guitars vibrate, the musicians sing a Congolese song in high-pitched voices, and you feel the throbbing in the pit of your stomach. You shake your hands and your legs, flinging everything all over the place. Your African partner is already in a world of her own, her face bearing an expression of not-knowingness. And the vibrations radiate from your stomach until your legs, your genitals, your chest, your brain — all are one mass of electronic rhythm. And the music swells and throbs. Time ceases to matter. All becomes a seething mass, like sperm in a release of semen.

The band plays for five, ten, fifteen minutes. When it stops, it starts off with another piece, hardly sounding different from the previous one.

You are already part of the whole pulsating universe. The whole electric universe. The whole orgasmic universe. Until the partner slowly withdraws, the vibrations recede. The music becomes too loud.

You see a couple next to you swinging away like a pair of brackets suspended on a clothes line in a heavy wind. You walk off the floor. Until the vibrations start reaching out again.

Dipping into the 'underworld', one was cleansed.

I did not go often to an African Nightclub, but tonight was an exception. I had had a rather unsettling day at the office. I had come to work half an hour late that morning and Mr Greene had let me have it. He had sent for me and ushered me into his office.

'Sit down, D'Souza.' He normally called me Deo. 'I've had enough of your sloppiness. Time and again, in spite of my warnings, you come in late.' He had previously joked about my latecoming. 'Your continued lateness is a reflection of general lack of concern about your work. You don't seem to think sufficiently before you send up your recommendations.'

He must have been referring to a minute I had written on the colonial Government's offer of loans to Damibia to meet payments of pensions and compensations that would be necessary as several expatriates would retire at Independence. I had expressed the view that the interest rates were too high, higher even than the commercial rates of interest. I had suggested that the Government negotiate with the colonial Government to reduce the interest rates since the civil servants were really the servants of the British Government and therefore, strictly speaking, the responsibility of the British Government. This seemed to have annoyed Mr Greene. Was he afraid that there would be no 'golden handshake'?

'I cannot tolerate sloppiness any longer. The next time you are late, I shall report the matter to the Permanent Secretary.'

'Yes, Sir!'

Inwardly, I was boiling. I hated Mr Greene, because I knew I was guilty of being late, probably the only Goan in the whole Civil Service who was ever late.

I had to dissipate my anger, like the scorpion that must sting something to get rid of its poison. Going to the Goan Institute would be of no use since inevitably the pattern of talk there was the Civil Service and its daily doings.

So I went to the New Jazz Nightclub.

And drank.

And danced.

I was just walking up to the bar after a dance when I saw this big black man sitting there. He saw me too and said, 'Hey Brown Man! What are you doing here? We don't get your kind here often.'

'I'm just enjoying myself.'

'And chasing African women! Why is it you Browns never bring your women to our nightclubs so that we can even the score?'

I had drunk too much and was still feeling sore. So I said,

'I'll tell you why, big man. We hate the crudeness and vulgarity of this kind of nightclub. Where nobody has any manners, the men are rough and treat the ladies roughly, the band plays too loudly and does not know when to stop. If you applaud the band after a piece, it takes you literally and plays the same piece for another fifteen minutes. The people dress crudely, and some even smell and get drunk. And most dances even worse.

'That's why we don't come here, big man. And that's why our women don't like to come here.'

The man was taken aback. So were the people around him. All conversation stopped. The silence was deafening. The man gazed at me for a long time. Then he said,

'Hey, barmaid, give my friend here a beer!'

He thumped me on the back.

'I like you, man. You're honest. You are the first Brown Man to answer my question directly, without being evasive. Come, let us talk.'

The hub-bub returned.

'What's your name, *Rafiki?*'

I told him.

'I am Robert Kyeyune. You may have heard of me.'

I had indeed! Robert Kyeyune was the foremost politician in the country. He had come into the limelight years ago. The workers of a foreign company that was the sole exporter of tea and coffee from Damibia had asked for a wage increase and had failed. Robert Kyeyune had organised a strike, during which he personally brought food for the workers from the countryside at reduced prices. The tea and coffee had started rotting in the sheds when the management of the company gave in and agreed to the wage increase. But Kyeyune did not stop there. He went on to organise the coffee- and tea-growers. He believed that the company was making exorbitant profits while the growers were being paid only a pittance. Under his leadership, the growers refused to sell their produce to the company or to any middle-man unless their prices were raised. The colonial Government locked Kyeyune up. The growers then increased their demands — even higher prices plus the release of Kyeyune. They also started burning their produce to prevent it being taken from them forcibly. Kyeyune was released and the growers received higher prices.

Later on Kyeyune had organised a very effective trade boycott in the largest county of Damibia against foreign firms and businesses. The purpose of this boycott was to force the government of Damibia to accept Damibians in the Legislative Council of the country. Again, he was locked up. But after the people did not buy anything from foreign businesses for two months, Kyeyune was freed and some

Damibians were taken into the Legislative Council — not Kyeyune, of course.

Lately, Kyeyune had aroused the ire of the colonial Government yet again. The colonial Government had already seen the writing on the wall, it had felt the wind of change, and it had now changed its tactics. Instead of denouncing Africans as savages incapable of ruling themselves, thus providing a moral basis for continued colonial rule, the colonial Government had now turned round and begun claiming that her rule had been one long training session so that the Africans could eventually rule themselves.

In the process, they were looking for 'good boys' who would play their game. They wanted 'responsible' African leaders in the Civil Service, business, politics and 'public life' generally whom they could build up into great men. They would then permit these men to get into power — and the 'Mother Country' would rule behind the scenes, with the co-operation of these good boys.

But Robert Kyeyune refused to play along. He seemed to be one jump ahead of the colonial Government. He publicly denounced its moves, saying that it had no intention of granting real independence. He said that it meant to grant fake independence so that Damibia could be controlled just as before by the Mother Country. The Government tried to suppress him without being too obvious. After his first letter was published in the local English paper, the Government introduced more stringent press censorship — indirectly, through the English editor of the paper. Kyeyune's subsequent letters were rather garbled, undoubtedly because they were published in a truncated form.

Kyeyune then started publishing his own newspaper in which he printed several items about which Africans were being wooed. I don't know how he did it; he must have had his own secret service, I suppose. Some of the individuals sued him for libel.

Have you seen a libel suit lost? For some reason, the courts seem to ignore the question of whether there is any truth in what is said but merely concentrate on whether something unpleasant has been said. Kyeyune represented himself and defended himself by proving he had written the truth. He fully documented his allegations. The libel suits were hastily withdrawn.

Then the Government started talking about the paper being 'subversive'. Once the businessmen found that the paper was subversive, they feared that if they continued providing the paper with advertising support, they would not obtain trading licences. So they withdrew their advertising support. The Banks withdrew their overdraft facilities. The paper collapsed.

Kyeyune then started making speeches all over the country. There were rumours that the Government was considering deporting him, as it had done to some prominent Africans years ago, or at the very least detaining him. But Kyeyune beat the Government again by throwing the spear first, so to speak. He told the masses that the Government wanted to deport him or detain him because he spoke the truth to the people, because he was not like the other African stooges who were willing to prostitute themselves and sell their own people. He said that the British wanted to leave by the front door and, while the *wananchi* were still waving goodbye, re-enter through the back door and tie everybody with fine but strong strings. In this, they would be assisted by their stooges. People like him would never agree to these evil plans and that is why the British wanted to detain or deport him. Kyeyune knew, of course, that the British were trying hard to project the image of training, guidance, etc. and would not want to upset the apple cart at this stage. And he was right — the British held their hand.

It was at this point that I met Kyeyune. To be frank, although I gave Kyeyune his due, I had distrusted him because I considered him a radical in the typical African manner. He claimed to be left-wing but did not confine his attack to mere systems: he also attacked the races and individuals who were part of those systems. He did not attack only Exploitation — he attacked Asian Exploiters. In the minds of most people, I was sure, Kyeyune was not condemning Exploitation but Asians. And what the leaders said today, the people would say tomorrow. So I only thought of Kyeyune as a rabble-rouser and did not have much respect for him.

All the same, had I known this was The Man in person, I would have been more polite! It is one thing to be critical of political figures in the abstract and it is another to be confronted by them in the flesh. There is something frightening about being face to face with a politician you know to be powerful. It is like suddenly coming face to face with a naked cable carrying 10,000 volts of electricity. Whether you like electricity or not, you know that one touch of the cable and you're dead or maimed.

The beer was served.

'Cheers!'

'Cheers!'

'What did you say your name was, Mr Brown?'

'Joseph D'Souza.'

'You're a Mugoa, eh? Not one of those Muindis.'

'Yes.'

'You're not one of the exploiters, then. You must be a Civil Servant.'

'Yes.'

'Are you an Accountant?'

'No, I am an Administrative Officer.'

'Are you really? Then you must have studied at University.'

'That's right.'

'Damibia University?'

'Yes. I graduated many years ago. I went abroad after that.'

'Where abroad?'

'Leeds University.'

'Hmm — one of those fiery, redbrick Universities! You must be a Socialist.'

'Yes, Comrade.'

'I like your style, Mr, M—'

'D'Souza.'

'Too many D'Souzas. Like the Musokes. No, I'll call you Mr

Brown. Abbreviated to Brown. I like your style, Brown. You're the first brown person I have come across to speak bluntly when asked a blunt question. The rest would have tried to evade the question, pretending that in Damibia, all the different races intermingled freely, as though we are all one people. Honesty of this kind is rare these days.'

I was lost for words. What does one say to a big politician, especially if one is an Asian? So at first I concentrated on drinking my beer.

'Barmaid! Another beer for Mr Brown here.'

'Let me offer you one—'

'Nonsense. Barmaid, are you deaf?'

God, what a capacity for drink Kyeyune had, like most Africans. Particularly beer. With me, the law of diminishing returns operates very early. This is one reason why it is difficult for an Asian to be sociable with an African. The barriers of race and social differences break down around the fifth beer, but most Asians cannot get beyond the third.

Around the fifth beer, the walls of the nightclub began closing in on me. Kyeyune loomed larger.

'Civil Service — how far do you think you will go . . . Principal Assistant Secretary? . . . The British won't let you go beyond Senior Assistant Secretary . . . your wide knowledge of politics . . . need an intelligent secretary . . . colour no bar . . . an asset . . . different perspective . . . one country . . . small but great . . . all coloureds exploited . . . JOIN ME—'

Kyeyune's face exploded.

I was a sputnik spinning round the earth. A thousand crazy woodpeckers were pecking on my metallic shell, the pecking getting louder and louder until I could bear it no longer. I started hurtling to earth.

Crash!

'Good morning, Brown.'

I was sitting on a floor next to a big bed, with a comfortable blanket round my legs.

Giant trees near my feet. I looked up the trees, and high up, saw a face — a black face, a familiar face.

'Ouch! My head!'

'Here, have this cup of African coffee, my friend. Yes, *black* coffee.'

I sipped the coffee and felt a little better.

'Where — Where am I? What happened?'

'Take it easy, Brown. You just fell off your stool at the New Jazz Nightclub last night. You could not get up. So I carried you here. This is my house.'

'Last night — what time is it now?'

'Mid-day, *Rafiki*.'

'Mid-day! !' I leapt up, and an invisible sledgehammer struck me on my head. I fell back. 'My head!'

'Come, come, Brown. Relax! You have to learn to take it easy! You know, you Asians don't know how to relax, although you have the economic means to do so.'

'But I have to get to my office. Mr Greene — my Head of Department — will give me hell for being so late! He's a stickler for punctuality!'

'But, my dear fellow, you have resigned from the Civil Service.'

'What — what do you mean?'

'Don't you remember — you agreed last night to quit the Civil Service and join me as my assistant.'

'WHAT!!!' The sledgehammer again.

'So I telephoned Mr Greene this morning, telling him to Go to Hell — which, to an Englishman, means Go home to England.'

I started retching, and was helped to the sink by Kyeyune, who was grinning his head off.

'You know, that's what you told me last night to tell your Mr Greene. You also told me to tell him that he was a colourless

84

bastard — which I did.'

Finally, I sank back, gazing at the ceiling.

'And now, you are my assistant, my secretary, my speech-writer.'

It couldn't be true. I couldn't have got into the crazy world of politics! Oh, I liked politics, but I preferred to watch it from afar. I must have impressed Kyeyune before collapsing . . .

'Look, Joe' — the only time he ever called me by this name — 'what the hell, excuse my French, is a fellow like you doing in the Civil Service? How much will you earn in the Service? After eight years, three thousand pounds per annum — if you're lucky.'

He went on to say that I could earn much more than that with him. He said that there were risks in the political world, but in any case, I probably would not live long enough to earn a pension.

'Look at me,' he said. 'My father was a polygamist. He ill-treated my mother, and she left him. She brought me up on her own, an illiterate woman, scraping a living from the soil so that I could go to school.'

He went on to say that I had no right to opt for security until I had had my share of risks. My head was still aching so I merely listened as Kyeyune asked me what I would contribute to the country by remaining in the Civil Service. In fact, I was already fed up with the Civil Service. It had built up a world of its own only remotely related to reality. I suppose to begin with, the Service had been in touch with the real world, but the words and procedures it had invented to cope with the world had taken on a reality of their own. The expression 'I have studied the matter very carefully' meant 'I have just skimmed through the matter a couple of minutes ago'. The phrase 'The matter is under review' is translated as 'Oh hell! I had forgotten all about it!' We civil servants used these magical words ritualistically until our minds went soggy.

And the Civil Service method of dealing with a problem! Say there is a shortage of water in a town called X, up-country. A Commission of Inquiry is appointed. The Commission consists of a group of mediocre officials who know nothing about water and couldn't care less. The officials make a trip to the troubled area, each in his own car so that he can get some mileage. I recall an older civil servant advising me when I was considering buying a car.

'Claim, do you hear, claim! If you make a trip to Darobi, claim! If you make a trip to Wamasonga, claim! If you make a trip to the Ministry of Housing a few hundred yards away, claim, claim, CLAIM!'

They all claimed whenever they could.

But if the water shortage was really in a remote area, nobody would want to damage his car. So instead, the officials would meet to discuss the problem. Some ideas would be put together and a draft report would be drawn up. In conclusion, the report would state 'After careful consideration, the Commission recommends that a borehole be sunk in X'. And every member of the Commission would be happy because the problem was being solved — a report had been drawn up!

The draft report is distributed to members of the Commission after three weeks, a meeting is called up in the fourth, postponed because the Secretary is away, and finally held in the fifth week. The report is finalised in the sixth week.

In the eigth week, it is discovered that X already had a borehole, which had gone dry. By that time, half the people at X are dead or have moved to other areas.

I felt I had come to a dead end in the Service. I had considered leaving, but was thinking of becoming a political journalist, not a practising politician. I was rather fond of my left-wing approach to political affairs. But somehow, I had not yet quit the Service. Kyeyune misunderstood my silence.

'Go back, go crawl back to your Mr Greene and say, "Big Boss Man, Sir, I'm very sorry that that crude African politician Kyeyune told you I was resigning. He lied to you, having made me drunk at the New Jazz Nightclub. I had gone there only to drown my sorrows after the slight misunderstanding you and I had yesterday. I deeply regret the matter, Sir. Please take me back, Sir." '

That annoyed me.

'Any African would be better than myself,' I said.

Kyeyune suddenly lost his temper.

'Don't oppose me!' he said. 'Am I a fool? You are an African. I know the kind of person I want. Too many "Africans" want to get rich quick and are willing to sell their souls to the devil — including the white devil. You will be loyal.'

I was beaten down.

'Okay, I'll join you,' I said.

'Good man, Brown!' Kyeyune simultaneously crushed my hand and broke my back. 'Come, let's have a drink on it. A beer!'

I must have turned green. 'Good God, no more beer!'

'I can see there's a lot I'll have to teach you, Brown!'

'But the thing is, I do not have enough —'

'You talk too much, Mr Brown. Cheers! Here's to a long and successful political relationship between us. Here's to our country, which is lucky to have sons like us.

'Here's to Real Independence!'

TROUBLE IN UGANDA

We had a lot of trouble in Kampala. We had no time to eat and also we had to pack our things in two days. We couldn't buy our tickets because we had to buy our suitcases and clothes.

We were eight people in our family and we had to buy suitcases for all of us and they cost three times more than they did before. For example, if a coat cost 100 shillings, the same coat cost 300 shillings after Amin told us to get out. The tickets cost 200 shillings each and we had to buy eight tickets; we borrowed 500 shillings from my uncle. And now we have to pay him back.

My father had to go to the office of the U.K. High Commission. He stayed there for about five hours and even then he didn't get a chance, because there was a queue about a mile long. My father didn't have time to eat. We also didn't eat our food because we were all worried how we could get everything done in only two days. We didn't sleep at nights.

We had to buy our things. We had to pack our things. My father had to get permission and buy our tickets. He also had to sell our car and send our parcels. Some people slept outside the U.K. High Commissioner's office and they also didn't get a chance. Some people went there brushing their teeth. There it was very hot and they had to stand in the queue under a hot sun all day. Their brains didn't work in the sun because it was very hot. Their skin became black in the sun. At the end my uncles helped my father to get the tickets and complete all the things.

In the airport many people fainted because of the heat and the crowds. The army at the airport killed many people. No one thought that they would be alive. We also thought that the army would kill us, but we were lucky. When we reached England, we all felt ill for a day because of the trouble we had had in Kampala. If anyone from Uganda thinks about this, he would just faint in a minute.

Virji Singdia (12)

MY IMPRESSIONS ABOUT ENGLAND

When I arrived here the first thing I noticed was the weather. It was very cold and foggy which is something we people had never faced before, because Uganda was much warmer. A few weeks back I saw some snow falling which I thought was just like cottonwool.

Manners here are quite diferent from ours. English people always use "please" when they want something and "thank you" when somebody gives them something. Our language is *Gujarati* and many people of our race do not know English.

The way of dressing is different. Here the women wear mini-dresses, trousers, maxi-skirts, hot pants and in the winter they wear warm clothes such as coats. Our dress is the *sarie* which is six yards long, though nowadays some women wear trousers and mini-skirts. In Uganda we never wore mini-skirts or hot pants because they were banned. We never had to wear warm coats and at first they were very heavy for us. The men wear the same dress as here.

The foods here are quite different. English people eat very little spices such as chillies, whereas we often eat them. The Muslims don't eat pork because it's against their religion, but all English people eat it. The Hindus don't eat fish or meat. Vegetables were very cheap in Uganda but here they are not. Fruits, such as apples, pears, grapes and oranges were very expensive.

Transport is the same as here except there are no underground tube trains. Here there are big and beautiful buildings whereas in Uganda there aren't many.

We go to pray usually on a Friday whereas English people go to church on Sundays. We have big occasions such as *Idd* and here they have Christmas. Marriage here depends on a girl finding a boy but we were not allowed to, although nowadays some of them are allowed. The rules here are different. A person over the age of sixty-five can get an old-age pension and free medical attention whereas in

Uganda people never get a pension. It is safe here because there are policemen to guard you whereas in Uganda we would never know when the Africans would come to rob us or kill us. Here the law says that a child should go to school until the age of sixteen while in Uganda the students would go to school for as long as they wanted or even not at all. The government here is very helpful.

This is all about my impressions of England.

Yasmin Jaffer (15)

PORTRAIT OF AN ASIAN
AS AN EAST AFRICAN
Jagjit Singh

I

the past has boiled itself over
and we are the steam that must flee . . .

i shall summon you therefore,
ancestral spirits of my race,
on this great issue of citizenship,
and you must plead before the minister
for being born so brown.

smile away the hurt of their unfriendly frown
for the sweat is dry
that built the railways,
and black blood must forget
swamp sleeping savagery of greenness
that burst into an indian bazaar,
because the time and tide
and the valour of your business mind,
condemned the brown jew
to comb his days in commerce and trade.

black blood of freedom
will soon break your bent shadow,
for you were the criminals of commerce
that daily sucked their coins across the counter.

now they shall look back in anger —
the mercedes-benz politicians,
black suited, whisky voiced, swiss bank accounted,
searching in vain
for brown liberals behind the counter
and taunt us about commitment —
for the blood is dry
that roused green savagery
from the slumber of the swamps.

and you will see it always,
in back alleys and government offices,
my subordinate asian smile of friendship
that proclaims the jew also is a citizen,
and the stare of past hostility replying:
citizen? . . . perhaps so,
but of asian extraction!

i must condemn you therefore,
ancestral spirits of my race,
for wrongful extraction also.

II

but my eyes shall burn again,
a resurrection of brown pride,
for i see you now, my father,
fling the victoria cross
into dung-heap of the british empire.

not for your valour
was this false honour on your chest,
but for blood discarded
and bodies dismembered
in white wars of yesterday.
why, then, must i,
your latter-day blood,
bow to live content
with vouchers and quotas?

III

farewell,
farewell my dear beloved illusions,
for, i, too, would have liked to think
only the toes of africa were infected,
but the cancer of colour
has gathered fresh victims now.

black surgeons, too, have prescribed new drugs
and we,
malignant cells,
must fade away soon.

let me not see you therefore,
ancestral spirits of my race,
in the posture of lawino
lamenting sweetness that has turned sour,
for it shall be my western mind alone
that must summon up an excuse
for the brownness of our sins.

and soon we shall be flying,
unwelcome vultures all over the world,
only to unsheathe fresh wrath
each time we land.

we are the green leaves
that must sprout no more,
for the roots have thrived
on black silence
and false kindness of the white race.

waste no ceremony
for the unintentionally corrupted;
lead the ram to the altar
and wash away the sins of history.

ON SPRING

The deep thought of my love
Under this new
And beautiful
Blue blue
Sky.

The glittering stream
Far in the distance
Reminds me of
Songs
Happiness
Telling me that winter is
GONE
And summer is just returning.

Kamal Kumar (13)